THOMAS FORD MEMORIAL LIBRARY

DEC   2008

W9-BYF-627

THOMAS FORD MEMORIAL LIBRARY
WESTERN SPRINGS, ILLINOIS

GAYLORD S

EXTREME SCIENTISTS™

BRAVING VOLCANOES:
VOLCANOLOGISTS

JUDY MONROE PETERSON

PowerKiDS
press™
New York

THOMAS FORD MEMORIAL LIBRARY
800 CHESTNUT
WESTERN SPRINGS, IL 60558

To Emmett and Owen

Published in 2009 by The Rosen Publishing Group, Inc.
29 East 21st Street, New York, NY 10010

Copyright © 2009 by The Rosen Publishing Group, Inc.

All rights reserved. No part of this book may be reproduced in any form without permission in writing from the publisher, except by a reviewer.

First Edition

Editor: Amelie von Zumbusch
Book Design: Kate Laczynski
Photo Researcher: Jessica Gerweck

Photo Credits: Cover, pp. 11, 13 © National Geographic/Getty Images; p. 5 © David Trood/Getty Images; pp. 7, 9, 15, 17 Shutterstock.com; p. 19 © G. Brad Lewis/Getty Images; p. 21 © Getty Images.

Library of Congress Cataloging-in-Publication Data

Peterson, Judy Monroe.
  Braving volcanoes : volcanologists / Judy Monroe Peterson. — 1st ed.
      p. cm. — (Extreme scientists)
  Includes index.
  ISBN 978-1-4042-4525-9 (lib. bdg.)
  1. Volcanologists—Juvenile literature. 2. Volcanological research—Juvenile literature. 3. Volcanoes—Juvenile literature. I. Title.
  QE521.3.P48 2009
  551.21092—dc22
                                    2008007738

Manufactured in the United States of America

CONTENTS

Hot Rocks

Did you know that rock can become so hot that it flows like water? Hot, melted rock called magma lies below Earth's surface, or outside. Sometimes, magma spills through a **crack** in Earth's surface and forms a volcano. Scientists who unlock the secrets of volcanoes are **volcanologists**.

Once magma leaves a volcano, it is known as lava. As lava flows on the ground, it cools off. Over time, the cool lava becomes hard rock and makes new land. However, lava can also kill people, animals, and plants. Luckily, volcanologists have learned enough about volcanoes to warn people when volcanoes are a danger.

Volcanologists take careful measurements of volcanoes to gain a better understanding of these important landforms.

Volcanoes and Earth's Plates

Earth's surface is made up of pieces called plates. These plates sit on top of magma and move between 1 and 6 inches (2.5–15 cm) each year. Volcanoes often form in places where the plates push together or pull apart. For example, several volcanoes have formed along the Mid-Atlantic Ridge, where plates are pulling apart the ocean floor.

Volcanoes come in different sizes and shapes. Some are tall mountains shaped like cones. These volcanoes formed from lava that flowed over thousands of years. Small, short volcanoes form when lava flows for only two or three days. Other volcanoes are just holes or cracks in the ground.

Popocatépetl, in Mexico, is a stratovolcano. Stratovolcanoes are steeply sloping volcanoes that were formed by big lava flows that happened hundreds of years apart.

Active Volcanoes

Today, Earth has more than 500 active volcanoes. These volcanoes regularly erupt, or shoot out lava. Sometimes, active volcanoes spit out **ash**, smelly gases, and small rocks, as well.

Many volcanologists work in places, or areas, with active volcanoes. One such area is the Ring of Fire. This 25,000-mile- (40,234 km) long belt of volcanoes circles the Pacific Ocean. The volcanoes are along the edges of a Pacific Ocean plate. About 350 active volcanoes are part of the Ring of Fire. That is more than half of the active volcanoes in the world.

DID YOU KNOW?

Washington's Mount St. Helens is part of the Ring of Fire. In 1980, this volcano erupted. A huge cloud of ash rose into the air. Sadly, 57 people died in the eruption.

Many volcanologists work in the Hawaiian Islands. These islands are home to several volcanoes, such as Kilauea, seen here.

What Do Volcanologists Do?

Some volcanologists study how lava moves or how a volcano grows. Other volcanologists study the dangers an erupting volcano can present to nearby people and land. Some volcanologists even visit volcano **craters** to study what volcanoes are like inside.

Volcanologists use tools, such as seismographs, to take measurements before, during, and after a volcanic eruption. Seismographs measure how much movement and shaking there is in the ground. Other tools measure how much the ground swells as magma moves under it. These tools help volcanologists predict, or guess, when a volcano might erupt.

DID YOU KNOW?

Volcanologists use a tool called a spectrometer to test gases from volcanoes. Smelly gases, such as sulfur and methane, give the scientists clues about when a volcano might erupt.

When they visit volcanoes, volcanologists often wear masks to keep them from breathing in bad-smelling or unsafe gases.

Unlocking the Secrets of Volcanoes

Volcanologists use many tools to study volcanoes. They often use tools called probes to collect magma and lava. Volcanologists then look at this magma and lava with special **microscopes** to discover what rocks and **minerals** are in it. When volcanoes are too unsafe to visit, scientists use **robots** to gather magma and lava.

The Volcanic Explosivity Index, or VEI, measures how strong volcanic eruptions are. Each blast is given a VEI number. This number takes into account how much lava, ash, and gas came out of a volcano during an eruption. It also takes into account how high the gases and ash rose into the sky.

Volcanologists often wear special clothes when they gather lava. Lava can be hotter than 2,000° F (1,093° C)!

Along with volcanoes, volcanologists sometimes study problems that volcanic eruptions cause. For example, when a volcano erupts underwater, large parts of the ocean floor are lifted up. This can cause giant waves called **tsunamis**. Tsunamis are very powerful. They can even destroy cities and towns.

Some erupting volcanoes cause **earthquakes**. The shaking ground can make buildings break apart and fall down. Earthquakes can set off landslides, too. This fast sliding of rock down a steep volcano can kill people, animals, and plants.

DID YOU KNOW?

When ash and dust from a volcano mix with water, a lahar, or mudflow, can form. In 1985, South America's Nevado del Ruiz volcano erupted. It caused lahars that killed 25,000 people.

Lakes sometimes form in the craters of volcanoes. Volcanic lakes are often very colorful, but they can cause lahars and let out clouds of unsafe gases.

Studying Old Volcanoes

Not all volcanoes are active. For example, a dormant volcano is one that has not erupted in some time but could erupt again someday. Dormant volcanoes are generally older than active volcanoes. Volcanoes that are completely finished erupting are called extinct volcanoes. Some extinct volcanoes look like tall mountains, while others have been worn down into hills by water and wind.

Volcanologists study the rock from old volcanoes. These rocks can give volcanologists clues about how land forms. Scientists also sometimes discover metals, such as gold and silver, in old volcanic rocks.

DID YOU KNOW?

One well-known dormant volcano is Mauna Kea, in Hawaii. Mauna Kea last erupted about 4,500 years ago. Lava from Mauna Kea's past eruptions helped form the island of Hawaii.

Oregon's Mount McLoughlin is a dormant volcano. Although it last erupted several thousand years ago, scientists think it might erupt again someday.

When Will This Volcano Erupt?

People once had no idea when a volcano might erupt. Today, volcanologists have learned ways to predict when an eruption is likely to happen. Before a volcano erupts, cracks in Earth's surface may widen. The ground sometimes swells up, too. Volcanologists measure these changes with special tools, such as tiltmeters and geodimeters. Small earthquakes often shake the ground before a volcano erupts. Volcanologists use seismometers to measure this shaking.

Volcanologists also use the Global Positioning System, or GPS. This ring of **satellites** flies high above Earth. The satellites send measurements about active volcanoes to volcanologists, letting the scientists know if the ground is moving or shaking.

The Hawaiian volcano Kilauea has been erupting steadily but slowly since 1983. Volcanologists track the lava flowing from the volcano and study cracks in its surface.

19

Saving Lives

When the volcanologists who have been studying a volcano think that it is about to erupt, they warn people living nearby. These warnings can save many lives.

For many years, volcanologists have watched and studied Mount Pinatubo. This active volcano is on the island of Luzon, in the Philippines. In 1990, volcanologists noted many earthquakes near the volcano. Early in 1991, the scientists recorded more earthquakes and saw white clouds of steam coming from the volcano. Lots of smelly gas came out, too. Volcanologists warned people living near Mount Pinatubo to leave. Many people moved to safer places. They were saved when the volcano erupted in June 1991.

Today, Mount Pinatubo is fairly quiet. A lake has formed in its crater. However, volcanologists watch the volcano carefully because they think it could erupt again.

You Can Be a Volcanologist

There are many volcanoes in the United States. You can visit some of these volcanoes. There are other ways to learn about volcanoes, too. Many **museums** and **universities** offer classes for kids to study volcanoes. Libraries have books and movies about volcanoes.

To become a volcanologist, you need to study math and sciences, such as chemistry and physics, in high school. Then, you will need to study **geology** at a university. Becoming a volcanologist takes hard work, but volcanology is a wonderful field. Volcanologists are always discovering new facts about our Earth. They keep cities and farms safe and save lives, too!

GLOSSARY

ash (ASH) Pieces of tiny rock that shoot out of a volcano when it blows.

crack (KRAK) A break or narrow opening.

craters (KRAY-turz) Openings at the tops of volcanoes.

earthquakes (URTH-kwayks) Shakings of Earth caused by the movement of large pieces of land called plates.

geology (jee-AH-luh-jee) The study of rocks and Earth's landforms.

microscopes (MY-kruh-skohps) Tools used to see very small things.

minerals (MIN-rulz) Natural things that are not animals, plants, or other living things.

museums (myoo-ZEE-umz) Places where art or historical pieces are safely kept for people to see and to study.

robots (ROH-bots) Machines made to do certain skilled jobs.

satellites (SA-tih-lyts) Spacecraft that circle Earth.

tsunamis (soo-NAH-meez) Waves caused by movements in Earth's crust on the ocean floor.

universities (yoo-neh-VER-seh-teez) Schools people go to after high school.

volcanologists (vol-kuh-NAH-luh-jists) People who study volcanoes.

3 1308 00263 7643

WEB SITES

Due to the changing nature of Internet links, PowerKids Press has developed an online list of Web sites related to the subject of this book. This site is updated regularly. Please use this link to access the list:
www.powerkidslinks.com/exsci/volcan/